RESTART

Philip
MURDOCH

RESTART
YOUR LIFE

LAN
PUBLISHING
WWW.EDILAN.COM

Rio de Janeiro, 2017
www.edilan.com.br

RESTART YOUR LIFE
by
PHILIP MURDOCH

© 2017 Philip Murdoch
Published by LAN Publishing
Richardson, Texas 75080
www.edilan.com

Printed in the United States of America

All rights reserved. No part of this publication may be reproduced, stored in a retrieval system, or transmitted in any form or by any means—for example, electronic, photocopy, and recording—without the prior written permission of the publisher. The only exception is brief quotations in printed reviews.
Unless otherwise identified, Scripture quotations are taken from the Holy Bible, New International Version®, NIV®. Copyright ©1973, 1978, 1984 by International Bible Society. Used by permission of Zondervan Publishing House. All rights reserved.

Please note LAN Publishing's publishing style capitalizes certain pronouns in Scripture that refer to the Father, Son, and Holy Spirit, and may differ from some publishers' styles. Take note that the name satan and related names are not capitalized. We choose not to acknowledge him, even to the point of violating grammatical rules.

ISBN: 978-1-945488-05-4

For worldwide distribution. Printed in the USA.

CONTENTS

Restart	7
Where Should I Plant the Mango Tree?	23
Ice Cream and Nutella	45
You Will Be Blown Away by What God Has Prepared	63
God Sees You through His Eyes	77
Explosion in the Garden	89
Have You Received Your Gift Yet?	99
Speed Up	109
About the Author	119

RESTART

A few years ago I bought an iPhone. I was a little hesitant at first because many of my friends who have an iPhone just couldn't stop talking about how fantastic, awesome, amazing and just absolutely brilliant the phone was. I knew that nothing in life could be that good. So, as an engineer, I took a look at the specifications before I bought it, and yes, it really did seem to be a good phone, but not exceptionally so. Its chip and processing speed were good, but other telephone companies, such as Samsung, offered chips and speeds of similar quality. And Samsung was even better in some categories. Also, the Apple's operating system (iOS) is closed, meaning that you can only use products and apps from Apple. For a thinking man like me, that sounded very backward, dumb, and even anti-democratic. However, all my cool friends, big-church pastors, and those friends I wanted to be like had an iPhone. They were cool. And I wanted to be cool too. So I did what millions of Apple users did — I gave in to peer pressure and bought the phone.

My first impressions were definitely positive. It had a solid and heavy feel, the design was amazing, and everything worked perfectly, all the time. It was really impressive. What's more, I felt that I also looked amazing when I was holding it. The iPhone had something special about it, something inexplicable. It changed the way I saw myself. It was like eating sushi. After all — let's be honest — who really likes raw fish? Sushi is much more than the food itself, it's about the whole experience of eating Japanese food, using chopsticks, and sometimes even sitting on the floor. It's cool. It's new. It's different. It's sophisticated. The iPhone was all that and more.

There are certain things which when added to something fantastic, make that almost perfect something even better. For example, a filet mignon steak! How can I improve on that? The answer is simple... by adding bacon! It is amazing how adding a slice of bacon to a filet mignon can make such a difference. The same is true about chocolate fudge. Everything is better with chocolate fudge. For me, the iPhone is what bacon is to filet mignon, or what chocolate fudge is to ice cream. I look good, but with an iPhone I look even better!

In fact, I started thinking that the phone was actually far better than my friends had described it to me. I started to use it and enjoyed everything about it, and I was ridiculously happy. I used the GPS, the calendar, and the weight-management and exercising app. I downloaded the app from my gym and the guitar tuning and decibel-levels app to control the sound volume at church. It was phenomenal and I was proud to be the owner of an iPhone — until something happened...

On October 5th, 2011, just a few months after I bought my iPhone, Steve Jobs passed away. Steve was Apple's founder and CEO as well as the main visionary of the company for many years. And just as I was starting to really like Apple, he dies. But the real problem came the next day: my iPhone stopped working! It simply froze! Was everything going to go wrong now that Steve Jobs had passed away?

I read the user manual, tried to play with the buttons — the button, I mean, because the iPhone has only one command button. I tried to shut down some apps and spent hours trying to make the phone work. Finally, I decided to call Apple technical support to ask for assistance. I had to wait for a short time, listening to music until it was my turn. At last I got to talk to someone who asked me, "Did you try to restart the iPhone?"

Restart? What is that? The assistant said that if I pressed the power button on the top part of the phone and at the same time held down the command button for 10 seconds, the phone would turn off. Then when it turned on again, everything would work as it was supposed to.

Restart! Great! I did that... First, everything shut down completely, but within a few seconds the Apple logo appeared in the center of the screen and after a few more seconds, the phone started to come back to life, returning to its original state as designed by the great master, Steve Jobs. A few seconds later, the phone started to work again — perfectly. It was not only working properly like on the day I bought it, but all the apps I had downloaded and the settings I had chosen were all still there. In other words, the *restart* had fixed everything that was wrong, without deleting anything that was right. All good and no wrong remained. Wow!!!

Did you know that turmoil, hardships, lies and strongholds in our lives tend to get so complicated that it seems impossible to improve, fix or get out of our situation? I don't know if you have noticed, but it looks like every time we fix one area of our life, ten other areas start to go down the drain. It seems as if we spend years trying to get our life in order when in fact we are just walking around in circles. Looking back, you ask yourself if there is more to life than this. As with the iPhone — when the only way to fix the problem is to do a *restart* — the answer to fixing our lives may be to just do a restart as well.

RESTART

Did you know it is
possible to press a button
in your life to have
everything restart too?

The great prophet Jeremiah once said,

> *The heart is deceitful above all things and beyond cure.*
> *Who can understand it?*
>
> Jeremiah 17:9

It is amazing that even Jeremiah, 2,600 years ago, could tell that our heart can be so unhealthy and so deceitful that it is in fact *"beyond cure"*. As human beings, we tend to try to fix it. In reality, we always want to fix the problem with the least possible effort. But as the great prophet Jeremiah said, issues of the heart cannot be solved by our weak attempts because it is *"beyond cure"*. In matters relating to the heart, a simple conversation with myself will not solve anything. Simply saying, "next time I will try harder" does not do the trick.

YOU NEED A RESTART

A few years ago, someone from our church called me at home and asked me to pray for her father who was in hospital waiting for coronary bypass surgery. As we talked, I began to understand her father's situation better. He had already had one heart attack, but none of his children knew that he suffered from any serious heart condition. His daughter continued talking, explaining that her dad had been to see a doctor the year before without any of the family knowing about it. The doctor had recommended bypass surgery, but her father never went through with it. At the time, he had gone to the doctor because he was feeling pain in his chest, but after doing all the emergency tests, the pain went away and he convinced himself that surgery was not necessary, even though the doctors strongly recommended it. He thought, "I know there is something wrong with my heart, but surely it is not bad enough to have to have surgery". A year later, he found himself once again in a critical situation. He was taken to hospital, but the doctors were unable to operate immediately because he was not in a stable enough condition for surgery. However, when his family visited him at the hospital, he seemed to be feeling much better and was even joking with his grandchildren while in the hospital bed. In their eyes, he had completely recovered. In his eyes, he had completely recovered, as he had many times before. However, the heart monitors told another story. Beneath his apparently healthy exterior, death was looming and the doctors continued to tell everyone that he was in critical condition.

Finally, after waiting for four days in the hospital, the doctors decided to go ahead with the surgery. He was laughing and joking as he entered the operating room, making light of the need for surgery. Nevertheless, the doctors insisted that his condition was critical and that the surgery, although possibly too late, was his only chance of survival. During the surgery, he had another heart attack, but this time it was fatal. His condition was too severe to withstand the additional strain of surgery and he died. As I talked with his wife and children, no one could understand how this could have happened, seemingly without any warning signs. Everything seemed to be fine at one moment, and the next moment he was dead.

That father's situation is no different from the situation many of us face every day. We know that

RESTART

Deep inside,
we know that there is a
decision, a new
direction that we
need to take

there is something spiritually wrong with our heart. We know that everything is not 100% well, but we also think it is not *that* bad. It is not bad enough to warrant action. It is not bad enough to change our whole lifestyle. Deep inside, we know that there is a decision, a new direction that we need to take, but at the same time, we convince ourselves that a total surrender to God would be too radical and unnecessary. Maybe going to church occasionally will solve it. Perhaps listening to a Christian radio station may help a little bit. Or buying a Bible and keeping it in the living room, or putting a bumper sticker on my car saying JESUS SAVES could be the solution. And all these thoughts get in the way of taking the only life-saving, life-transforming medicine — a new, renewed and changed heart.

Today you are in the process of pressing the restart button to renew your life and to be born again. If you have the courage, we can press that button right now while reading this book and everything that was wrong, unbalanced and out of order — literally everything — can get back on track to God's perfect plan.

I invite you now to press that button for 10 seconds and to come back to God's perfect plan

If you have the courage,
you can press that button
right now and everything
that was wrong, unbalanced,
out of order — literally
everything — can get back
on track to God's
perfect plan.

and purpose for your life. This requires boldness. You will have to admit that the way you have lived has not been working and that the direction you are walking in will not take you to the perfect destiny and powerful purpose that God has for your life. That's why I invite you to read the following Bible verse and to pray the Restart Prayer:

> *Therefore, if anyone is in Christ,*
> *the new creation has come:*
> *The old has gone, the new is here!*
> *All this is from God,*
> *Who reconciled us to Himself through Christ.*
>
> 2 Corinthians 5:17-18

RESTART PRAYER

Lord Jesus, thank You for the message in this book. I have heard many people talk about You and I want to believe that You can really be all that and more for me too. I know that my life has not been going in the right direction. I have sinned. Please forgive me and come into my life and press the restart button so I can live 100% of Your plan and purpose for my future.

Thank You and Amen.

WHAT GOD IS SAYING TO ME:

_____
_____
_____
_____
_____
_____
_____
_____
_____
_____
_____
_____
_____
_____

WHERE SHOULD I PLANT THE MANGO TREE?

It is interesting how we are all so different. I am the kind of person who doesn't like to have fixed routines. I like every day to be different. But when it comes to the daily life at home, I would prefer to have everything continue the same. My wife, Renée, on the other hand, is the opposite. She doesn't like sudden changes in her routine. She likes to wake up at the same time every day, go to bed at the same time every night and have a daily exercise routine. However, when it comes to our home, she constantly wants to paint a wall a different color, rearrange the furniture and she loves gardening, which from my point of view means my having to move plants around. For me, personally, all that is somewhat irritating.

I remember a specific event years ago. Renée wanted to buy a mango tree for our garden. In my opinion, our garden already had plenty of plants and trees, but she didn't think so… she needed more, many more. Obviously, I had to be involved because, in her mind, I was going to be the one to dig a hole and plant the tree. So I got my shovel and walked up to the spot where the mango tree was going to be planted. I remember specifically asking her, "Are you <u>sure</u> this is the best spot?" She said yes, so I started to dig, and dig, and dig. Finally, after more time and sweat than I had anticipated, I managed to plant the tree. Phew! Thank God, it was done! Renée was happy and I was happy that she was happy. I went back into the house to take a shower and do what I do best: watch TV.

A week later, Renée brought me again to the spot where I had planted the tree. The tree was clearly having a hard time adapting to its new habitat. In my view, the tree would eventually adapt really well, but Renée said, "This spot doesn't get enough sunlight." Then she told me to dig up the tree again and move it to the other side of the garden to a better spot with more sunlight. After complaining just a little, I soon agreed to do what she was asking. This time the task required double the work since I had to dig it out of the ground, fill in the hole, then dig another hole at the new location and plant it again! Finally, I was able to do it all, and the mango tree was in its new location, this time with plenty of sunlight and everything seemed to be fine.

Another week went by and, once again, one of my greatest fears came true. Renée called me out into the garden again and said that the tree was now being exposed to too much sunlight and it couldn't be watered properly because it was too far from the hose. She convinced me to move the poor mango tree again. I did what she asked and moved it to where there was sunlight and also close enough to the hose so that "we" could water it. The following week, Renée realized that the soil where the tree was now planted had once been a construction site and the soil was full of rubble. We couldn't see the rubble because it was covered by topsoil. However, I knew she was right because as I dug the hole to plant the tree I found huge chunks of concrete and rebar. This both depleted the nutrients, as well as affected the pH of the soil, so ... I had to move it again.

Finally, as a result of repeated planting, uprooting and replanting, all the leaves fell off and the mango tree died. We had tried so hard, but there seemed to be something not quite right about every place we had planted the mango tree. There just didn't seem to be any perfect place for it. At the same time, every location that we planted it also had many good qualities. The problem was that we couldn't enjoy the blessings of any of the locations because we constantly focused on the inadequacies.

Did you know that many people face a similar situation in their church life? They keep church hopping because they are always looking for a little bit more perfection. They are constantly focusing on what is wrong and not on what is right! By doing this, they miss out on huge opportunities for growth and spiritual advancement.

The problem was that we couldn't enjoy the blessings of any of the locations because we constantly focused on the inadequacies.

RESTART

If a tree is planted and uprooted repeatedly, do you think it will thrive and flourish?

If a tree is planted and uprooted repeatedly, do you think it will thrive and flourish? Will it bear fruit? Will it be beautiful and productive? Will that tree become everything God has planned for it and fulfill 100% of God's destiny? I don't think so.

> *Those who are **planted** in the house of the Lord,*
> *Will **flourish** in the **courts** of our God.*
>
> *Psalm 92:13*

This scripture shows us an amazing link between being planted and flourishing in the courts of our God. What are the key words for learning in this scripture?

- Planted
- Flourish
- Courts

Planted: Just as in the analogy of the tree, our lives also demonstrate many of the same characteristics. We also need a constant diet of spiritual food so that we can grow. No church is perfect, and no place will have the perfect conditions without any shortcomings. Nevertheless, God calls us to be planted in His house. If you have the courage, let me make a suggestion that I think will greatly help you reach all that God has in store for you.

Determine in your heart that you will remain planted in your church for at least six months. During those six months, involve yourself in as much as you can. Find out the central vision of your church and be bold. Talk to the leaders about how you can dive in, and find out what practical next steps you can take. Your leaders may ask you to take one or more classes, or to go to a few meetings, or to get involved in a small group. For sure, you will have to be faithful to attend the church services. As Nike says, *just do it!* Don't give up if there is an unexpected detour or obstacle on the way. Don't get discouraged if the first person you speak to seems to forget about your request. Persevere! After all, we are talking about your future, your pathway to becoming and doing all that God has lined up for you. I am confident that you will begin to see real growth in the spiritual aspects of your life. In fact, see this as a test and I assure you: in six months you will look back and will be blown away by everything God has done in and through your life.

Flourish: the second word is *flourish*. Jesus invested much of His time preaching and telling parables about seeds, plant growth and fruit. In John 15, Jesus even said that God is glorified when we bear much fruit.

> *In His words, "This is to My Father's glory, that you bear much fruit, showing yourselves to be My disciples"*
>
> *(John 15:8).*

Bearing fruit, or flourishing, is an important part of our new walk. God has already prepared everything, but you have to take action and allow the miraculous to flow in your life.

God has already prepared
everything, but you have to
take action and allow the
miraculous to
flow in your life.

Jesus loves us regardless of how much fruit we produce, but His purpose and the way to real satisfaction and eternal happiness are obtained through bearing fruit. There is an amazing Bible verse that talks about this:

> *For we are God's handiwork, created in Christ Jesus to do good works, which God prepared in advance for us to do.*
> *Ephesians 2:10*

Just as a growing and flourishing tree depends on several variables, we also need certain essential factors in order to flourish. A few of them are constant water, soil with good nutrients and protection so that we are not trampled on. All of these can be found in your church.

That brings us to the last word:

Courts: Nowadays the term 'courts' has more to do with sports than protection. However in biblical times, the term 'courts' has a significant meaning in many books of the Bible. Back then, the royal residential palaces were built with a fortified wall around them. This wall protected a beautiful, fruitful internal garden. The fortified wall was equipped with weapons of attack and defense to protect the royal family's residence and the beautiful garden of fruit trees and flourishing plants in the inner court. No one could enter the inner court without first gaining entry through the fortified wall.

For example, the book of Esther tells us that the queen wanted to talk to the king, but she was not allowed to because he was in the inner court. At that time, no one could approach the king while he was in the inner court, unless specifically summoned to do so. If anyone, including the queen, were to enter the inner court without being invited, they would be killed, unless the king held out his scepter giving his permission to enter the court. Today, the court still exists. It is a beautiful place of protection and fruitfulness. It is a place where shade and refreshment can be found. It is a place where all the members of the king's court can flourish and bear wonderful fruit, a place where there can be unobstructed growth allowing everyone to fulfill 100%

Today, the court is
the house of God.
The court is the
church.

of their potential. Today, the court is the house of God. The court is the church. Read the scripture once again and allow this truth to saturate your mind and soul.

> *Those who are planted in the house of the Lord, Shall flourish in the courts of our God.*
> Psalm 92:13 (NKJV)

Just as it is with a royal court, occasionally there is internal intrigue in the church too. As time goes on, we may face conflicts or have misunderstandings with other people. A survey was conducted in the 1980s about American missionaries working in Africa. The survey attempted to discover the main reason missionaries were returning to the USA earlier than planned. In other words, why were the missionaries not succeeding in their ministry work? There were many hypotheses. For some, it may have been the lack of financial support. For others, it could have been the extremely difficult living conditions in Africa. Or maybe it was being exposed to tropical diseases, such as malaria, yellow fever, dengue or other debilitating and life-threatening illnesses. Some missionaries may have preferred to return because they could not find suitable schools for their children. Others may have had difficulty adapting to cultures with political instability or wars… or perhaps it was just the accumulation of many seemingly minor things that when added up became overwhelming.

No. The survey showed that none of these was why missionaries gave up and returned to the USA. The main reason was interpersonal conflict with other missionaries. Think about it! Members of the same team fighting with each other was the main cause for failure in the mission field!

In my experience, I see the same happening in the church. The main reason why people tend to leave a church is not because of typical difficulties, but because of conflicts with other people who are part of the same team.

Take a look at this scripture in Ephesians 4:16,

*From Him the whole body, **joined** and **held together** by every* *supporting ligament, grows and builds itself up in love, as each part does its work.*

YOU NEED TO BE JOINED

The key words in the verse above are *"joined"* and *"held together"*. These two words in the original, and before the New Testament was written, were terms more commonly used in the context of construction of homes, especially with regard to carpentry. The word *join* describes the slot carved out of two wooden beams so they can fit together. For example, a slot is cut in one of the beams and another slot is cut into the other beam, so they can be joined together. One Bible translation[1] even calls it *"fitly joined"*.

In the church, it's not enough to just come, listen and leave. What we hear needs to be put into practice and, more often than not, significant adjustments need to be made in our lives. Some

---
[1] King James Bible

may call this discipleship, but one of the main reasons God put you in the church is to enable adjustments in your life, to *join* you with others. Interestingly, the main tool God uses to make these adjustments is your relationship with others. That is why whenever you are irritated by someone in the church, it's very likely that God is using that relationship to make adjustments in you. He is carving a slot out of your life, so that you can be better adjusted and fit into His calling. I know this does not sound all that encouraging, however, take comfort that God is using you to make adjustments in the other person's life too! ☺ So, if we run away, leave or avoid deepening our relationships, we run the very real risk of not making the adjustments we need and therefore not achieving all of God's plan for our life.

Some people say that the church is a building. Others say the church is people. The truth is that the church is neither a building nor people. Once, I invited a very famous Christian singer to our church. It was amazing the size of the crowd that that singer drew. However, I soon discovered that those people were not the church. The following

Sunday the same old congregation was there. All the new people had gone to see the next big show. If I were to invite Justin Bieber to sing at our church, it would be crowded out as well, but those people would not be the church. The church is made up of *connected* people.

During the construction of a house, various building materials are used to build walls, pillars, the roof, ceilings and other parts. Yet, there is always stuff that needs to be thrown away at the end of the construction: the construction debris. Did you know that people who say they go to church, but are not *connected* — with each other and with God — are like construction debris? They are at the construction site, but play no useful part in the construction itself and, at the end of the project, the clean-up crew comes along and sweeps them all away. In some places, they may even make a big bonfire to get rid of all the unwanted, useless, old building materials. You need to allow God's adjustments in your life so that you can get really connected, and those adjustments can only happen in the church.

The church is neither a
building nor people.
It is made up of
CONNECTED
people.

YOU NEED TO BE HELD TOGETHER

The second key word in the verse is "*held together*". Just like *joined*, the words *held together* also come from terms more commonly used in the context of construction. The term refers not only to the cut made to connect two beams, but also to the *process* of connecting them.

Back when the New Testament was written, they didn't use nails and glue to connect wooden logs. The best way to create a connection between the beams was to make a very precise, tight and compact splice. By the way, one of the translations of the term *held together* is 'compact'. When two wooden beams are joined, they need to be compacted in order to fit together perfectly. Have you ever felt that a relationship in the church is compacting or pressuring you? We all have had that feeling and we should thank God for building His house through compacting, adjusting, joining and holding our lives together with other lives.

Now, I invite you to get *planted* in a church and to *flourish* in the *courts* of His protection in order to fulfill 100% of your calling and potential through your relationship with others in the church.

RESTART PRAYER

Father, thank You for the amazing opportunity to be planted in Your church, that is, Your body. Come into my life and give me time and boldness to become firmly involved in the vision of my church. Holy Spirit, develop my spiritual life so that I can grow to fulfill 100% of my potential in Christ.

Amen.

RESTART

WHAT GOD IS SAYING TO ME:

ICE CREAM AND NUTELLA

All human beings have something in common: habits and addictions. There are innumerable studies by psychologists about habits and addictions, but the overall conclusion is that when we start to do something repeatedly, our mind creates a chemical conditioning that gives us the predisposition to do that same thing over and over again.

One of those studies was done in 1998 by Judith A. Ouellette and Wendy Wood, and was published in the Psychology Bulletin. It proved that an account of past behaviors could predict future behaviors with a high degree of certainty.

All human beings have something in common: habits and addictions.

I have clearly seen that in my own life. For instance, as a pastor, I have many meetings which end late in the evening and I often get home after my wife and kids have already gone to bed. A few years ago, I started to — occasionally — prepare a bowl of ice cream when I got home. And since there was nobody looking, I would decorate the ice cream with a generous amount of chocolate syrup and sometimes even condensed milk. Staring at that bowl of ice cream, I thought it was still lacking something. So I found the Nutella, and put a large dollop of it on top. Now I had a perfect midnight snack!

To begin with, it was only a small problem. However, it became a big problem when the "occasional" became "often" and the often became "daily" and daily became an expectation. The situation got so bad that sometimes I would be in a meeting praying for someone and my mind would start thinking about the ice cream sundae instead of the person for whom I was praying. I would try to end the meeting hurriedly because my mind was saying, *Philip, your midnight snack… GO BACK HOME,* **REMEMBER THAT ICE CREAM WAITING FOR YOU***…*

I know you are probably shocked by my confession, especially because I am a pastor. After all, how can a pastor confess that he is thinking about ice cream right while he is praying for someone? Please forgive my honesty, but the truth is that all of us have a propensity to condition our lives to habits and even addictions that have the ability to control how we live. These addictions can be found in many areas of our lives. For instance, during an especially meaningful moment during a church service, our minds might start thinking about a football game, or an Indy Race, or a TV show, or dinner, or a girlfriend — all these things can become addictions that can shift our focus from the Holy Spirit to our own lives. We need to wake up and really understand the spiritual battle that is going on. What is the eternal value of a football game or an Indy race or, for that matter, ice cream?

Some people have addictions with regard to their emotions. Every time they hear something that doesn't please them, they pout or sulk. They stop talking to that person for days or even weeks, or respond aggressively.

Addictions can also influence our eating habits, as I described above. Some addictions have consequences that are potentially even more destructive, such as the type of websites we access, or our drinking habits — or other damaging, self-destructive actions.

The important thing for our health is that we recognize that those addictions and habits end up controlling, or at least directing, our lives. I don't know about you, but I think it's ridiculous to allow a bowl of ice cream to control my life. I just declare right now: Enough of being a slave to repetitive actions and wrong thoughts in my life! Slavery was officially abolished in 1865 in the United States, but it seems I am still captive today.

Read the following scripture:

> *It is for freedom that Christ has set us free.*
> *Stand firm, then,*
> *And do not let yourselves be burdened again*
> *By a yoke of slavery.*
>
> Galatians 5:1

Christ came to abolish addictions and habits that control you and to set you free from your former way of living. What was Jesus thinking? What advantage did He have in setting us free? What difference does it make to Him?

Addictions blur our vision. Instead of seeing everything God has prepared and all He has planned for us, our vision is consumed by our addiction. While I, as a pastor, was supposed to be thinking about the person for whom I was praying at the altar, my thoughts were focused on my bowl of ice cream. There is nothing more powerful to take us away from the path God has mapped out for our lives than physical and emotional addictions.

This is what I think: Jesus knew that if you could be truly free, you would be able to see everything around you clearly, without being enslaved by addictions and habits that blur your vision. In Jesus' mind, when we are truly free we will choose the best for our lives. And His plan, purpose and destiny are always the best for us. The truth is that even though psychology teaches us that past behavior predicts future behavior with a high

The truth is that even though psychology teaches us that past behavior predicts future behavior with a high degree of accuracy, it doesn't need to be true in your life because of the power of the Gospel. You don't need to be a statistic!

degree of accuracy, it doesn't need to be true in your life because of the power of the Gospel. You don't need to be a statistic!

> *So if the Son sets you free, you will be free indeed.*
>
> John 8:36

> *But whenever anyone turns to the Lord, the veil is taken away. Now the Lord is the Spirit, And where the Spirit of the Lord is, There is freedom.*
>
> 2 Corinthians 3:16-17

The best way to be free from addictions is by introducing new and good "addictions" into our lives. In Matthew 12, Jesus told a story about a man who was set free from a demon. The story says that after a period of freedom, the evil spirit found seven other spirits more wicked than itself and returned to occupy that person who had been set free.

Thus, we learn that long-lasting freedom is not only about removing evil, but also about intentionally filling our life with good. With that in mind, I have prepared three simple daily habits we need to develop in our lives.

1. DAILY PRAYER AND BIBLE READING

For many years, I have worked planting churches throughout Brazil. That has brought me great satisfaction, but not without difficulties. The greatest difficulty in church planting is the loneliness pastors feel. This is especially true of pastors who plant churches in outlying, distant locations. They often feel isolated, solitary and alone. This feeling is always a huge blow to their personal motivation and, occasionally, they become so discouraged that they even give up their calling.

Something similar happens to new believers. When you don't develop a lifestyle of communication with God, you end up feeling distant and isolated. The Father wants to speak to you daily, and that happens through prayer and reading His Word. I suggest that you dedicate a specific time of the day to connect with God. Personally, I think that the earlier in the morning the better. Find a place in your home and start by simply talking to God. Even if it is only for five minutes, it is already a good start and you will have five more minutes with God than most other believers have in a week!

Besides that, I would like to challenge you to read the Bible. My challenge for you is to read the entire Bible this year. I especially recommend that you find a one-year Bible reading plan. There is a free plan on YouVersion that is available in both Android and IOS versions. Each day you will read a scripture from the Old Testament, Psalms, Proverbs, and the New Testament. Many of the reading plans in YouVersion also include a devotional that will help you understand what you are reading. For many years, I have been reading Pastor Larry Stockstill's One Year Bible Devotional. The short devotional summarizes all those scriptures in such a way that you end up carrying these thoughts and meditations throughout your day.

The Father wants to speak to you daily, and that happens through prayer and reading His Word.

2. THE SECOND ESSENTIAL HABIT FOR YOU TO DEVELOP IS *FELLOWSHIP WITH OTHER BELIEVERS*. GOD NEVER WANTED YOU TO LIVE ALONE.

> *And let us consider how we may spur one another on toward love and good deeds, not giving up meeting together, as some are in the habit of doing, but encouraging one another—and all the more as you see the Day approaching.*
> Hebrews 10:24, 25

God has purposely created in you the need to learn from other people. You need a church that will encourage you and where you will find good friends.

3. THE LAST ESSENTIAL HABIT TO ENABLE YOU TO REMAIN FREE IS *SERVICE*.

> *Sitting down, Jesus called the Twelve and said, "Anyone who wants to be first must be the very last, and the servant of all."*
> Mark 9:35

God has purposely created in you the need to learn from other people.

You will only develop your calling when you begin to serve. And you will only develop great gifts when you allow those gifts to germinate as a seed and then grow. Talk to your pastor and ask his permission to serve in some area. Don't think he will let you preach immediately, but allow yourself to be used by the Lord as a servant and let Him promote you at His pace. Trust that He will be in control if you allow Him.

Today I invite you to take a bold step to recognize the veil of addictions and habits that control your life. Only Jesus can set you free! Receive the Holy Spirit in your life and let the veil of blindness and addictions be removed. Let the Lord pour down a destiny of freedom over your mind, body and spirit.

You will only develop your calling when you begin to serve.

RESTART PRAYER

Jesus, thank You for the freedom You have conquered for me through Your sacrifice on the Cross. I confess that I do have addictions and habits that control my life. I have tried to break them, but I honestly don't know if I have the ability to do so. Today I receive Your freedom. Please give me the strength to never go back to a yoke of slavery. And Lord, help me to develop habits of praying and reading Your Word, of fellowship with other believers and of serving You and Your church.

Amen.

WHAT GOD IS SAYING TO ME:

YOU WILL BE BLOWN AWAY BY WHAT GOD HAS PREPARED

One of man's most powerful characteristics is optimism. Optimism has the ability to influence many people to persevere even when they are facing great adversities.

I love the quotes from Winston Churchill, the great English prime minister, who led England to resist, fight and eventually defeat the Nazis, against overwhelming odds. One of my favorite quotes is:

The pessimist sees difficulties in every opportunity.
The optimist sees opportunity in every difficulty.

There are indeed two basic types of human philosophy. The first says the future holds dangerous uncertainties from which I need to protect myself, so best hunker down. The second says the future is better than the past. I can hardly wait for tomorrow.

When you add faith to optimism, we find an amazing, explosive combination. In fact, the very nature of faith always has to do with the future. Jesus told a story about a father with two sons. Some pastors call this story the parable of the prodigal son. Both sons had the same father, lived in the same house, and had been brought up under very similar circumstances. However, their perspective on the future couldn't have been more different. The youngest son was constantly looking to the future with optimism and expectation, and the oldest was constantly looking to protect what he had from the past. The youngest son would say:

You Will Be Blown Away by What God Has Prepared

The pessimist sees difficulties in every opportunity.
The optimist sees opportunity in every difficulty.

- I will get my inheritance.
- I will go to a distant land
- I will work for a foreign man
- I will arise
- I will return to my father
- I will repent and say to my father…

On the other hand, the oldest son focused constantly on the past:

- All these years I worked like a slave
- All these years I never disobeyed you
- You never gave me even a small goat to celebrate with my friends
- This son of yours wasted all your wealth

It is interesting that even though the youngest son did many things that were wrong, the gist of the story seems to suggest that the father was more pleased with him than with the oldest son who apparently was far more "good." To me, one of the clear messages in Jesus' story is that a constant look to the future with optimism is something that pleases God. Of course, I am not suggesting that faith has to do with self-confidence;

Faith says that everything I am going through,
or that I have gone through,
is preparing me for a better future.

however looking to the future with positive anticipation of the fantastic things that God has prepared for us is indeed one of the initial steps of faith.

The optimist thinks, "This is the best church in the world." The pessimist says, "What a drag! I think he is right! I will never find a better church than this dump."

The optimist is enthusiastic about what he possesses. The pessimist gets depressed thinking about what he will never have.

The optimist says, "This is amazing!" The pessimist says, "I expected more."

The Bible teaches us the concept of faith. Faith always has to do with the future. Faith never looks to the past. Faith says that everything I am going through, or that I have gone through, is preparing me for a better future.

In October 2012, I suddenly received the worst possible news. The police in Rio de Janeiro, Brazil, called me to tell me that a man had attacked my beautiful wife, mother of my four little kids, using a wooden fence post. He had hit her head so hard that he had cracked her skull into several pieces and literally cracked it from the top of the head all the way done to her jaw. She immediately went into coma. At the very moment I received the news, she was undergoing brain surgery with a team of young Brazilian interns trying to save her life.

How can we have faith when confronting such bad news? Later on, that same day, the doctor showed me a computerized prognosis of a possible recovery process for Renée. It was based on a study of more than 10,000 patients in different countries and the hospital where she was having the surgery had been included as part of that study. According to the research, Renée had only a 28% to 42% possibility of survival during the next 14 days. However, the really bad news was that if she did survive, she would have a 88.6% to 93.8% probability of being so seriously injured that she would have to be hospitalized for the rest of her life. In other words, she had an almost 94% likelihood of having irreparable brain damage.

As an eternal optimist, I concluded that she would still have a 6% chance of complete recovery. Again, the doctor felt it was his responsibility to lower my expectations of a positive outcome. Put another way, he wanted to kill my optimism — kill my faith. He explained to me that in the very unlikely event that Renee survived the first 14 days and performed better than the 94% of patients that would have severe brain trauma, she would most certainly have at least some form of lasting neurological consequences. These could include not being able to walk, talk, remember, see or hear.

Upon hearing all this, I tried one more time and asked the doctor what the chance of total recovery was. He said that in the medical field there is always a possibility for anomalies in the statistics. From his point of view, it is what laymen such as me call miracles, but in his opinion, these exceptions were so rare they are not worth mentioning, and that I should prepare myself for the worst.

Many of my friends and pastors started to tell me not to listen to the doctors, because they would weaken my faith. But my faith was not being weakened. The doctors had one level of truth. They had the ability to see up to a certain extent, but true faith can see further. I don't believe we should be afraid of bad reports, or a negative perspective from a doctor, lawyer or accountant. I think it is our duty to listen to them. They are not lying to us. They are telling us the truth. However, their perspective is merely natural.

Faith is not limited by earthly reality. Earthly reality is propelled and changed by the truth of faith. Faith is not seeing less, but seeing more.

Faith gives us an additional dimension to truth. Faith is not limited by earthly reality. Our earthly reality is propelled and changed by the truth of faith. Never feel that your faith will be diminished by listening to others. Faith is not seeing less, but seeing more! I could see and understand what the doctors were telling me. However, I could also see and understand something that was beyond what they could see or understand.

With that in mind, I decided to look at the medical report with my head held high and with the understanding that the doctors knew only part of the truth, but through faith, I would be able to see a more complete truth.

You will surely have your faith tested at some point in your life. I hope it is not as traumatic as the test I just described, but I know that we are all tested. What is important to understand when you are going through a time of testing is that the best is yet to come. Your future will be abundantly better, bigger, more prosperous and more motivating than your present. Trust God and dive deep into every single wonderful day God gives you.

You Will Be Blown Away by What God Has Prepared

However, as it is written: "What no eye has seen, what no ear has heard, and what no human mind has conceived" — the things God has prepared for those who love Him."
1 Corinthians 2:9

I almost forgot to tell you how my wife's story ended. Yes, she recovered completely. She went through six brain surgeries, followed by two years of neuropsychological recovery. She is driving again and has recovered 100%. She is in the category of the less than 1% of patients with brain trauma who have recovered completely. Even her doctor said that we can use the word *miracle*. Today, Renée travels the world preaching and ministering about her testimony, and sharing her book *"It's a Beautiful Day"* *(LAN Publishing* 2016), because nothing is impossible for God. It is amazing how her life has changed and how God used this awful, horrific attack to bring amazing healings to many. At all of Renée's meetings, we constantly see testimonies of people healed from cancer, other diseases and even addictions.

RESTART PRAYER

Lord Jesus, thank You for having amazing plans for my life. Thank You so much that I don't have to live my life hiding and running away from difficulties, because You have given me the ability to go through any and all situations with my head held high, a brave heart, and confidence in Your victory. I surrender all my life into Your hands completely.

Amen.

YOU WILL BE BLOWN AWAY BY WHAT GOD HAS PREPARED

WHAT GOD IS SAYING TO ME:

_____
_____
_____
_____
_____
_____
_____
_____
_____
_____
_____
_____
_____
_____
_____
_____

GOD SEES YOU THROUGH HIS EYES

There are two types of people on Earth: those who constantly worry about what others are thinking about them, and those who couldn't care less about what others think. Both types of people have strengths and weaknesses.

As a pastor, I see this a lot in church. At times, I see couples who are obviously going through serious difficulties in their marriage, but when they come to church, I see the husband open the door for his wife, and treat her with kindness and respect in front of everyone. Yet, no one knows that on their way to church in the car they had a huge argument and exchanged words that couldn't even be written in a book like this, which is sold in Christian bookstores. How can people change so radically when they think others are watching them?

Personally, I have always felt self-conscious about my weight, or should I say my "overweight"? Although I have recently invested money in a gym membership, have a TV program called *Spiritual Personal Trainer*, and have fasted quite regularly, even so, the circumference of my waist has constantly expanded. As I am concerned about how I look and haven't been able to reduce my weight consistently, I have developed some techniques in an attempt to disguise or cover up my inadequacies.

For example, I started wearing a jacket when I preach. I don't know why, but in my mind, the more clothes I have covering my belly the better. Also, when I am being filmed, I always make sure that they film me from my chest up in order to avoid showing my worst physical attributes. It's unbelievable, but I have even developed a technique in which I shrink my belly when taking photos. The problem is that, besides not being able to breathe properly, I end up looking very uncomfortable in the photos. In all the photos, I have that weird, strained smile that makes me look like I am not being sincere. Of course, I am not being sincere, I am hiding my belly. The truth is that I am way too concerned about what others may think of me.

The heart of the problem is that my concern is about what people think of me and I am not concerned enough about what God thinks. After all, what does God think about me? What does God think about you?

> *God made Him who had no sin to be sin for us, so that in Him we might become the righteousness of God.*
> 2 Corinthians 5:21

Think about this scripture. It is amazing! We know that we all sin and have unending flaws, but even so, in God's eyes we are His righteousness!

If I were to ask you to describe God's righteousness, you would probably use words like total justice, perfection, goodness. God's righteousness is not a conditional, temporary or partial righteousness. God's righteousness is complete. Incredibly, in His eyes, that complete righteousness is manifest in our lives. In fact, the scripture says that we are that righteousness.

In the book of Ephesians, we find the famous passage about spiritual armor. We see a list of the parts of the armor we should wear and use. One of them is the breastplate of righteousness. The breastplate was made of two pieces of leather or metal that the warriors wore over their chest, abdomen and back to protect themselves against the enemy's attacks. (Based on the anatomical geography of my body, I would need a custom-made breastplate.)

The breastplate has many interesting aspects. First, it was impossible for a warrior to put on the breastplate by himself. Someone else had to put it on for him. They would hang both parts of it over his neck, then tie them, or even screw them together. In the same way, our breastplate of righteousness can only be used because Jesus conquered that access for us. He tied up our righteousness. We could never have put it on by ourselves. Secondly, the breastplate was rigid and didn't allow much

Others may see you that way,
you may see yourself that way,
but God sees us through
His eyes:
the eyes of righteousness.

movement of the chest and abdomen. I don't know if you have seen depressed, sad people. Even their physical posture seems to be depressed, down and despondent. With the breastplate of righteousness, it is impossible to look down. It forces your head to be held high. That is, even if you wanted to look down, it would be impossible while you were wearing the breastplate, because it makes your back straight and requires you to look straight ahead, chest puffed out and head held high. That's how the breastplate of righteousness also works.

I constantly hear people with a wrong understanding of God's vision of us say, "I am only dust", or "I am a miserable sinner", or "I am not useful", or "I'm dumb, ugly, stupid", or even worse things. Maybe these descriptions are truly how you see yourself. Maybe they might even be how others see you. But is this really how God sees us? Does God see people as dust, dumb, ugly or stupid? I really don't think so. After all, He made us. Even though others may see you that way and you may see yourself that way, God sees you through His eyes: the eyes of righteousness.

The Bible says that we all have sinned and have fallen short of the glory of God, and that all of us are dust and to dust we will return. But how does God see us? As miserable sinners and dusty wretches? No! God sees us as people who were like that in the past, but even so, He still pursues us in order to develop a relationship with us. While we were still sinners, Christ died for us (see Romans 5:8). He sees us as people who once were lost living in depravity, but He sent His Son to die for each one of us.

God created us out of dust, but doesn't see us as dust because He breathed His eternal Spirit into the dust of our lives and transformed that dust into abundant life.

God sees us as His complete righteousness.

> *Therefore, there is now no condemnation for those who are in Christ Jesus, because through Christ Jesus the law of the Spirit who gives life has set you free from the law of sin and death.*
>
> Romans 8:1-2

This is my question for you today: What is the correct way to see yourself? Should you see yourself as others see you? Or should you see yourself as God sees you?

The answer is obvious: We need to see ourselves the way God sees us. The only way we can fulfill everything He has for us and start walking and accelerating on the path He has prepared for our lives is by seeing ourselves through His eyes. We are God's righteousness.

The problem is: how can we continue believing that we are God's righteousness when we know that we sin and often walk against His purposes and the best choice for our lives?

> *My dear children, I write this to you so that you will not sin. But if anybody does sin, we have an advocate with the Father — Jesus Christ, the Righteous One.*
> 1 John 2:1

We need to see
ourselves the way
God sees us.

Yes, we are God's righteousness. God sees us as His righteousness and we should also. When we deviate from His path, we should immediately return to the Father's arms, repent and trust that the merciful power of Christ is interceding for us when there is sin.

RESTART PRAYER

Lord Jesus, I don't even know how to fully describe how much I am thankful for You and Your mercies in my life. I know I have lived far from what You have planned for me, but You still see me as Your righteousness. I ask You to transform my life, my mind and my emotions so that they will conform to Your will. Help me to live my life purely and correctly, and at the same time give me access to a life free of judgement, self-condemnation and depression.

I put on the breastplate of righteousness, lift up my head, and look happily into the amazing future You have prepared for me.

Amen.

RESTART

WHAT GOD IS SAYING TO ME:

EXPLOSION IN THE GARDEN

We recently went to our church retreat where my youngest son spent a lot of time with the youth. As we all know, teenagers like to walk right up to the limit of what is permitted. Some of the church youth had brought fireworks to set off in the evening. Ethan, my son, was very excited about the "edginess" of doing something that was almost wrong and got together with all the other boys to set off fireworks and do what every boy likes to do… have fun.

On our way back home in the car, Ethan showed me one of the firework bombs the boys had given him. I was also a teenager once and I also loved fireworks as a boy, but I had never seen one that big. I tried hard to restrain myself and not show my son that I was afraid when I saw it. It was huge! It was thick, long, and heavy — really scary. I immediately told my son that he could not set it off because it was very dangerous. Ethan kept insisting and we finally came to an agreement: I would set off the firework together with him.

Well, I ended up forgetting about our conversation, but a few weeks later, we hosted a party at our house and Ethan came up to me and asked if we could set off the firework bomb together. There were about 20 new members of the church at our house, people I really wanted to impress. I wanted them to have a good impression of my family, the church and myself. It was about eight o'clock at night and it was a particularly dark night. Although I didn't feel too good about what Ethan wanted to do, I finally succumbed to the pressure and agreed. While he was holding the firework, I explained that I was going to light the wick and as soon as it was lit, he should throw it to the ground. Everything was OK — we understood each other.

So he held out his arm holding the firework and I lit the match and placed it under the wick. It took longer than I would have expected for the wick to begin to burn and make that characteristic crackling sound, but it finally did. It was scary to see the size of the firework bomb in my son's hand. I guess all my lecturing him about the dangers of fireworks took effect because as soon as the wick caught fire, instead of throwing it to the ground, he threw it way up into the air and over in the general direction of my neighbor's house! In my mind everything came to a halt and I began to see everything in slow motion. I saw the lighted firework go up and up and spin around and around in a huge arc of fire towards my neighbor's hedge. The arc finally began to descend and the firework fell into a bush, preventing it from landing in the neighbor's back yard. It was a beautiful bush with red flowers, one of Renée's favorite bushes. It was dark outside and I could see an ever-increasing glow in the bush and a great amount of smoke rising from it. In a panic, I started to think about what I could do to extinguish the burning bush. I felt like an inverted Moses! Instead of a burning bush that was never consumed, I saw Renée's favorite bush being consumed at an extraordinary speed.

BOOOOOM!!!!!

The firework bomb finally exploded and blazing leaves shot up into the sky. After a few seconds, flaming leaves and twigs started to rain down all over my yard. The guests stopped what they were doing and watched everything, probably thinking, "Wow, this is the best party at a pastor's house I've ever been to. I didn't know pastors were allowed to do that. Cool!!!"

I, on the other hand, panicked, trying to figure out all the other possible outbreaks of fire that would need to be extinguished when the blazing leaves landed. In the end, there were no other outbreaks of fire — God had mercy on me, my family, and the neighbor's house. The next morning, the burning bush in my yard had become half a burned out bush.

Interestingly, the word the Bible uses to describe the power of the Holy Spirit is a word which is similar to dynamite, or bomb. That word is found 120 times in the New Testament and describes the power of the Holy Spirit moving through Jesus and through people as well.

Amazing! Jesus wants to
work in our lives
with a power which is
comparable to an explosion
of life, freedom, testimony,
miracles and growth

*[He] who is able to do immeasurably more than all we ask or imagine, according to His **[explosive] power** that is at work within us.*

Ephesians 3:20

Amazing! Jesus wants to work in our lives with a power which is comparable to an explosion of life, freedom, testimony, miracles and growth. Just as the firework bomb that my son set off scared me, the power of the Holy Spirit is scary too. But at the same time and in the same way as my son's bomb attracted me, so the power of the Holy Spirit also attracts me.

*But you will receive **[explosive] power** when the Holy Spirit comes on you; and you will be My witnesses in Jerusalem, and in all Judea and Samaria, and to the ends of the Earth.*

Acts 1:8

The reason why so much religion appears to be boring and powerless is that it is boring and powerless! The power of our new relationship with God is developed through a relationship with the Holy Spirit of God. He, living in us, releases an abundance of supernatural, explosive power in our lives.

I invite you today to dive in and submerge in a new wave of God's flow. If you haven't been baptized in water, obey the Bible and be baptized in water as soon as possible. However, also ask the Lord Jesus to baptize you with the Holy Spirit, with the evidence of God's explosive power operating in your life.

> *Which of you fathers, if your son asks for a fish, will give him a snake instead?*
> *Or if he asks for an egg, will give him a scorpion? If you then, though you are evil, know how to give good gifts to your children, how much more will your Father in Heaven give **the Holy Spirit** to those who ask Him!*
>
> Lucas 11:11-13

RESTART PRAYER

Lord Jesus, I believe and desire everything You have prepared for me. I believe You want to baptize me with the Holy Spirit and with fire. And I receive this explosive power and baptism in the Holy Spirit with arms wide open and a thankful heart.

Amen.

WHAT GOD IS SAYING TO ME:

HAVE YOU RECEIVED YOUR GIFT YET?

I have always been really bad at giving gifts. I never remember birthdays, not even my children's or my parents' birthday. It is definitely one of my flaws. I try to get it right, but I usually fail badly. When I remember to buy a gift, I don't know what to buy, so I end up buying a boring and predictable gift.

I remember many years ago, while Renée was pregnant with Julia, our first daughter, I wanted to give Renée a special gift. In fact, I wanted to give her her very first Mother's Day gift. It had to be something expensive, and that would have a lasting impression. My goal was to buy a gift that Renée would never forget and that would really help her daily routine.

We lived in the States back then, in a house with an immense backyard. We had twenty-one big oak trees in our garden. The garden was usually covered with leaves and it was hard for the grass to grow because it was constantly in the shade. Two of the trees were over 100 feet tall and were less than 12 inches from our house. Huge branches from those trees had already fallen onto our roof twice, damaging the shingles and even breaking the battens. On one of those occasions, we didn't have the finances to fix the broken roof, so I bought some plastic sheeting and stapled it over the damaged part of the roof. A few weeks later, we started to hear noises coming from the attic. I finally had the courage to go up with a flashlight to see what was going on. To my surprise, I found three raccoons living there, a mom and two baby raccoons. While Renée and I both love wildlife, we don't appreciate it inside our home. We set a trap with fruit to capture them, but all we caught was a possum. The raccoons were still there. Our attic had become a zoo, or better yet, Jurassic park.

Renée constantly complained about the raccoons in our attic, so I thought, "I know what I will get her for Mother's Day!" I went out, bought it and wrapped it up. And on Mother's Day, I gave her my surprise. It was a…

CHAINSAW

My reasoning was that the gift wasn't actually for her to use (I'm not that crazy), but I could borrow it and cut the trees down.

Did you know that God has given and made available a vast range of amazing gifts for you too? But there is a small important detail. Just as the chainsaw was given to Renée as a gift, but it was for me to use — so the spiritual gifts God has given you are not exactly for you either. They are for you to use in order to bless others, the church and the Kingdom of God.

That reminds me of someone who was a member of our church years ago. He was exactly the kind of man every pastor wants to have in the church. He was a high capacity business leader who was very interested in getting involved in the church. There was just one small problem. He was very vocal about protecting HIS ministry, HIS anointing, HIS gifts. At the beginning, his verbiage sounded OK, but after hearing the words "my ministry" and "my gifts" over a thousand times, I started to get annoyed. Finally, I told him that his gifts were mine and my gifts were his. The Bible teaches us that we are given spiritual gifts to help one another.

You have gifts that God prepared for you. I encourage you today to begin your journey of discovery in order to identify and develop those gifts. Nothing in your life will satisfy you more than receiving a gift from God and seeing how He moves through you to help others.

Over the years, many people have asked the magic question: What is my purpose? The truth is that it is very difficult to jump directly into discovering our purpose. However, there is a somewhat easier way of coming to the same conclusion. For example, if we were able to understand what we are truly like, then we might be able to understand

What is my purpose?

what we were made for. The idea is something like this: if God created me in a unique and exclusive way, and if He created me for a unique purpose, then if I can find some of the specifics of what I am like, then I will be able to better understand what He created me for.

> *For we are God's handiwork, created in Christ Jesus to do good works, which God prepared in advance for us to do.*
> Ephesians 2:10

Think about this. The Bible says that God has given everyone — including you and me — a specific set of spiritual gifts. If we are able to identify what those gifts and unique personality are, then we might be able to begin to understand the purpose He has for our life.

> *Follow the way of love and eagerly desire gifts of the Spirit...*
> 1 Corinthians 14:1

The duty of discovering your God-given gifts is really yours. The Bible teaches us to eagerly desire spiritual gifts. Thus, I encourage you to buy books that talk about the gifts you find interesting. Ask your pastor about the best way to discover your gifts and how God created you in a unique way to fulfill His fantastic plans. Try to find other people who operate in the same gifts as you, and stay close to them so you can improve, train and refine your gifts.

RESTART PRAYER

Lord Jesus, thank You for the spiritual gifts You have prepared and given me. Also, thank You for entrusting those gifts into my hands so that I can help Your people and Your Church. What I most desire is to be used to bless lives. Help me to discover my gifts, develop them, and use them to help others.

Amen.

Have You Received Your Gift Yet?

WHAT GOD IS SAYING TO ME:

_____
_____
_____
_____
_____
_____
_____
_____
_____
_____
_____
_____
_____
_____

SPEED UP

Years ago, I read an account about the life of the incredible physicist, Albert Einstein. Many consider him one of the most brilliant minds in human history. He developed several theories that were not even able to be proven for many years. Only decades later, appropriate tools were developed to test and indeed prove those brilliant theories.

Einstein had a highly prolific time in his youth. He graduated from high school at 15, from college at 17, and earned his doctorate at 26. During that time, he published many significant works. His famous *Theory of Relativity* and the E=mc² equation were also published when he was 26. One of the most noteworthy aspects about Einstein was his rapid intellectual progress. However, just as rapidly as he grew in intellect, so also it came to a sudden end. No one knows exactly what happened, but in an almost scary way, Einstein stopped having enlightened thoughts.

In 1952, Einstein was offered the position of president of Israel, but he refused it. Some of his childhood friends report they were disappointed that Einstein didn't continue developing brilliant ideas, and instead spent most of his time sailing rather than inventing. In other words, Einstein's best and most productive years were the first 26 years of his life.

Similarly, in the Bible we see Moses rapidly progressing in the first few years of his life. He was educated by the best teachers in Egypt, which was the world's superpower at that time. When he was 40 years old, Moses committed a terrible mistake that apparently derailed his whole life. He murdered an Egyptian army officer and had to run away to the desert for 40 years. To the natural eye,

Moses' life was over. No one heard about him, no one saw him, people no longer thought about him.

Nonetheless, after an encounter with God, Moses rose up from the ashes. He was given a command from God and once again became a leader of God's people with a mission to lead Israel from slavery to freedom.

These two stories lead us to a question: Are your best years over or are they yet to come?

> *She is clothed with strength and dignity; she can laugh at the days to come.*
> Proverbs 31:25

This passage in Proverbs describes the attitude we can have about our future: look and laugh! Your future is going to be amazing, but I want to encourage you to constantly try your best to grow in the spiritual aspects of your life. Read the Bible daily, invest time in prayer and hearing what God has to say about your life, dive into the center of your church's vision, and

These two stories lead
us to a question:
Are your best years over, or are
they yet to come?

desire with all your heart to improve and develop your God-given spiritual gifts.

I want to end this simple book by reminding you that there is no adventure better, richer, more valuable, and more exciting than your walk with the Lord Jesus. Your future will be better, more powerful and more tremendous than you can imagine.

Hold on tight because God will speed up your life!

Your future is going to be amazing!
I want to encourage you to constantly try your best to grow in the spiritual aspects of your life.

SPEED UP

RESTART PRAYER

Lord Jesus, I know that the best in my life is yet to come. Help me to have the courage to run this race with all my heart. Help me to look ahead with a smile on my face, to wake up every day filled with strength and excitement about the challenges and victories in my future. Lord Jesus, help me to live a life of faith.

Amen.

WHAT GOD IS SAYING TO ME:

ABOUT THE AUTHOR

Philip Murdoch and his wife, Renée, are missionaries who have worked in Brazil since 2000. They are also the senior pastors at Light to the Nations Church, which has many campuses across Brazil. They have four children: Julia, Micah, Caroline and Ethan. Philip travels extensively throughout Brazil and around the world speaking to leaders. He is also the author of the following books: *"Till Marriage Do Us Part"*, *"Almost Everything You Want to Know About Sex, Dating and Marriage"*, *"Spiritual Personal Trainer"*, *"Church Planting Manual"* and *"It's a Beautiful Day"*.

WHAT GOD IS SAYING TO ME:

WHAT GOD IS SAYING TO ME:

_____
_____
_____
_____
_____
_____
_____
_____
_____
_____
_____
_____
_____
_____

WHAT GOD IS SAYING TO ME:

WHAT GOD IS SAYING TO ME:

Made in the USA
Columbia, SC
09 October 2017